PATRIOTIC SYMBOLS

The Statue of Liberty

Nancy Harris

Heinemann Library
Chicago, Illinois

Customer Service **888-454-2279**

Visit our Web site at **www.heinemannlibrary.com**

Photo research by Tracy Cummins
Designed by Kimberly R. Miracle
Maps by Mapping Specialists, Ltd.
Printed and bound in China by Leo Paper Group

10 09
10 9 8 7 6 5 4 3 2

10 Digit ISBN: 1-4034-9382-0 (hc)   1-4034-9389-8 (pb)

Library of Congress Cataloging-in-Publication Data
Harris, Nancy, 1956-
   The Statue of Liberty / Nancy Harris.
      p. cm. -- (Patriotic symbols)
   Includes bibliographical references and index.
   ISBN 978-1-4034-9382-8 (hc) -- ISBN 978-1-4034-9389-7 (pb) 1. Statue of Liberty (New York, N.Y.)--Juvenile literature. 2. New York (N.Y.)--Buildings, structures, etc.--Juvenile literature. 3. Signs and symbols--United States--Juvenile literature. I. Title.
   F128.64.L6H364 2007
   974.7'1--dc22

                              2006039384

Acknowledgements
The author and publisher are grateful to the following for permission to reproduce copyright material: ©Alamy **pp. 6** (nagelstock.com), **12** (CW Images); ©Corbis **pp. 5** (flag, Royalty Free), 14 (Free Agents Limited), 15 (Bettmann), 16 (Richard Hamilton Smith), 17 (Reuters/Jeff Zelevansky), 23 (Reuters/Jeff Zelevansky), 23 (Richard Hamilton Smith); ©Getty Images **pp. 5** (quarter, Don Farall), 8 (Ezra Shaw), 9 (Joe Raedle), 10 (Hulton Archive), 11 (CSA Plastock), 18 (Romily Lockyer), 20 (David Turnley), 21 (Royalty Free); ©istockphoto **pp. 5** (Liberty Bell, drbueller), 13 (Klaas Lingbeek-van Kranen); ©Shutterstock **pp. 4** (Ilja Mašík), **5** (White House, Uli).

Cover image reproduced with permission of ©Corbis (Sygma/Michel Setboun). Back cover image reproduced with permission of ©Getty Images (Royalty-free).

Contents

What Is a Symbol?

The Statue of Liberty is a symbol.

A symbol is a type of sign.

A symbol shows you something.
A symbol can have words.

The Statue of Liberty

The Statue of Liberty is a special symbol.

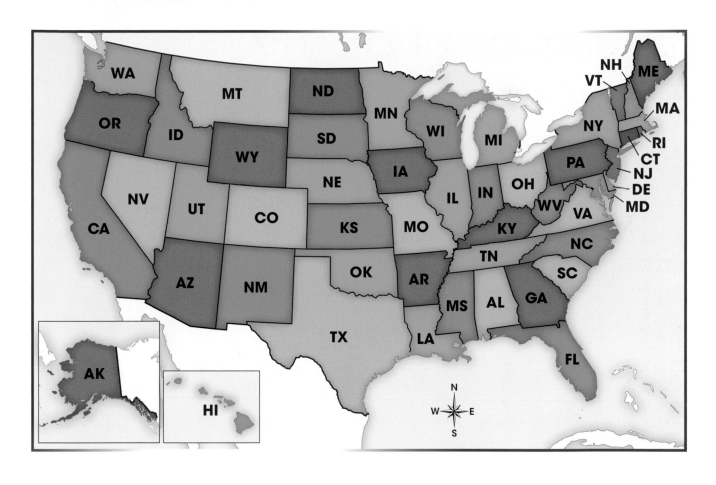

It is a symbol of the United States of America.
The United States of America is a country.

The statue is a patriotic symbol.

It shows the beliefs of the United States.
It shows the belief in freedom for all people.

France

The statue was a gift to the United States.

It was a gift from France.

France is a country.

Torch

The statue holds a torch.
A torch is a light.

The light is a symbol.
It stands for freedom.

Book

The statue holds a book.
The date on it is July 4, 1776.

The date is a symbol. The date is when the
United States became a free country.

Broken Chains

The statue has broken chains.

The broken chains are a symbol.
They are a symbol of freedom.

Crown

The statue wears a crown.

The crown has seven spikes.

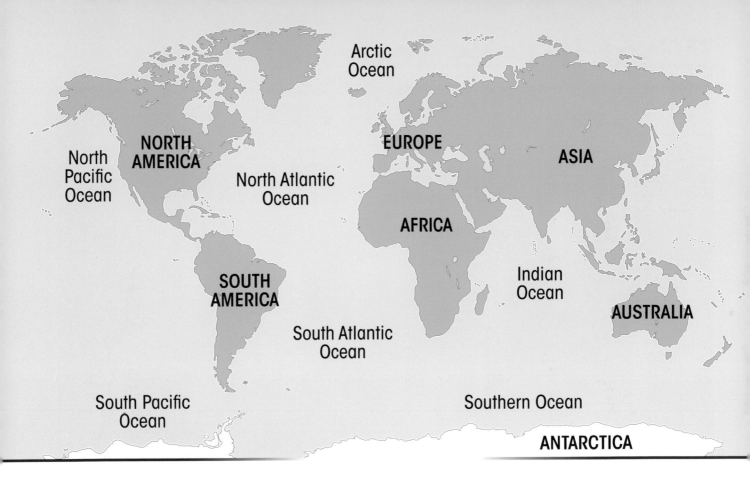

The spikes are a symbol of the 7 seas.
They are a symbol of the 7 continents.

What It Tells You

The statue is a symbol of freedom in the
United States.

The statue is a wish for freedom around the world.

Statue of Liberty Facts

★ The Statue of Liberty is in New York City.

★ The Statue of Liberty is a woman.

★ The torch does not have a flame.

Timeline

✪ The Statue of Liberty was given to the United States in 1885.

✪ The Statue of Liberty was opened to the public in 1886.

Picture Glossary

 **chain** metal band that can be used to imprison someone

 **continent** a large area of land

 **country** an area of land that is ruled by the same leader

 **patriotic** believing in your country

Index

Note to Parents and Teachers

The study of patriotic symbols introduces young readers to our country's government and history. Books in this series begin by defining a symbol before focusing on the history and significance of a specific patriotic symbol. Use the timeline and facts section on page 22 to introduce readers to these non-fiction features.

The text has been carefully chosen with the advice of a literacy expert to enable beginning readers success while reading independently or with moderate support. An expert in the field of early childhood social studies curriculum was consulted to provide interesting and appropriate content.

You can support children's nonfiction literacy skills by helping students use the table of contents, headings, picture glossary, and index.